Emerald Mandala

Emerald Mandala

Musings of Mind and Spirit

J. MICHAELS

RESOURCE *Publications* · Eugene, Oregon

EMERALD MANDALA
Musings of Mind and Spirit

Resource Publications
An Imprint of Wipf and Stock Publishers
199 W. 8th Ave., Suite 3
Eugene, OR 97401

www.wipfandstock.com

ISBN 13: 978-1-60899-096-2

Manufactured in the U.S.A.

To all of those souls
who mistakenly think they're alone

Contents

Preface xiii

The Emerald Mandala 1

Conscious Denial 2

Large and Magnificent 3

Vocation Vacation 4

The Healing 5

We Three 6

Unspeakable 7

Holding the Pen 8

Eventual Demise 9

Favorite Words 10

My Course 11

Of a Single Density 12

Much to Gain 13

Vortex Spit 14

A Maker's Dozen 15

All the Same 16

Center's Heart 17

Most of All 18

Fool's Errand 19

Absolutely Pure 20

So 21

By Way of J 22

Singing Love 23

Brothers Forever 24

Something Worth Talking About 25

A Struggling Time 26

The Body is Nothing 27

Staying Blind 28

A Dark Idea Diffused 29

I'll Live Until I Don't 30

The Greatest Lie 30

Dignity 30

Dark Corners 31

Masquerade 32

No Fear 33

Towards Beauty 34

Let Me See 35

Little or Nothing to Pay 36

A Willing Part of the Whole 37

At Love's Simple Request 38

Casey's Game 39

Chains of Our Own Making 40

A Bolt Once Thrown 41

Nowhere Outside Heaven 42

The World's Fool 43

Poet's Quarter 44

I Speak Only of You 45

Freedom's Press 46

Always on Time 47

Waiting 48

Hot Off the Press 49

Divine Fortunes Untold 50

Elusive Rhyme 51

Magic Flute 52

I Make No Apologies 53

As Gentle as Jesus 54

Guilt Jail 55

Holy Family 56

I, Not Me 57

Become the One 58

How I Do It 59

The Greybeards 60

If Only We Understood It 61

Faith to See 62

The Best Map 63

Never Look Back 64

Buckle Up Buttercup 65

Quite Right 66

Times Left Blue 67

Colored in White 68

Jammin 69

Full Sails 70

Attention to Innocence 71

No Need to Travel 72

Mystery of Rhyme 73

Fading Laws 74

Incomplete Facts 75

Leaving the Dream 76

Cranky 77

Beauty of the Thought 78

Ego's Dirge 79

My Babies 80

Daily Bread 81

The Golden Ring 82

Normal Sanctuary 83

Full Attendance 84

Lack of Contrivance 85

Light Breezes 86

Nothing Left to Say 87

Lost Without You 88

Our Best 89

Multicolored Space 90

Genius in Many Forms 91

Me2 92

Two Guests 93

Home Song 94

Unlimited Field and Stream 95

Captain of the Oar 96

Love Delivered 97

Table Laid Lightly 98

Portrait of the Whole 99

Street Smart 100

Far Less Separation 101

Journey Unlike the Rest 102

Song of Prayer 103

Til I Die 104

The Imaginerium 105

Integrating in Time 106

Part and Parcel 107

We 108

Departed 109

The Futile Joining of Two 110

The Constant Challenging of Reality 111

Mon Frere 112

Amid the Joy 113

Holy Grail 114

Sight Bereft 115

It 116

The Size of the Gift 117

Without Life's Pain 118

The Flower 119

Be Remembered 120

The One From the Two 121

Become Golden Hearted 122
Heaven's Milk 123
From the Past 124
We Choose 125
Chest of Gold 126
The Answer 127
No Pain, My Gain 128
Places Outside the Origin 129
I Awake This Morning 130

Preface

THIS WORLD WE CALL home, is not. We label it that. We assume it is all there is. But we're wrong, dead wrong. And although we may not know exactly where *home* is, something deep inside tells us this just isn't it. Call it emptiness, a hole in the soul, quiet desperation, or just feeling lost. We have all known that feeling at sometime in our lives, if not for the entire duration of our stay in this place that plays host to bodies. We all know it and we all search for that *something better*, even if we don't have a clue what that *something better* is. God knows, we try a million different things in the pursuit of it. From the feminine breast and the urge to go back to the womb, to competition in all our efforts, money and all that it buys, to sex, fame, and power. We numb ourselves with drugs, distract ourselves with entertainment, pollute our minds with pornography, and deafen ourselves with sound. We pursue pleasure in its myriad forms hoping, always hoping, to find the one thing that will fill us, make us whole, and make life meaningful. And while we pursue, we distance those close to us, we dilute our self-respect, and we distort our souls.

If we get lucky along the trail, we find another lost soul or two who helps us survive and find our way. It may be in the most improbable of places, it may be with the most unlikely of people. But somehow, something happens and we are given opportunities to self-correct our course, a chance to look in a different direction. For me, that was two people; a very good friend and a wonderful woman who became my wife. The good friend has moved on, as can happen in life. But he was there when my vain pursuits had deposited me at the depths of my existence. His love and caring friendship gave me hope and pulled me from the drowning depths. As I said, he has since moved on and I truly miss him and the times we had together. But that's okay. That's the way life works sometimes. God sends us angels in many forms and once their work is done, they may need to move on.

The second angel who graced my life was my wife. When we first met, I'm not sure who was in the worst shape. She had hit bottom, I had hit bottom, and we started out with a relationship that certainly did not appear to be made in Heaven, but it was. Twenty years later, here we both are and our partnership has grown to be an enriching and fertile ground for spiritual growth. She has been essential to every important moment in my life over the last twenty years and I will continue to thank God for her until the day I leave this worldly stage.

There have been many others. They have come and gone and sometimes I have recognized their value and sometimes not. To those fair souls, I tip my hat. In fact, I tip my hat to all of my brothers and sisters for what we have all brought to each other, known or unknown. I truly believe there is not a single one of us who has been left untouched. Whether or not we realize it, or acknowledge it, or value it, is another thing altogether; they were there. They were there with the right words, a hug at the right time, or an unselfish devotion to a friend in need.

Several years ago, my wife/angel gave me a book. That book was titled *A Course in Miracles* and it became exactly that to me, a course in miracles. After realizing what a gift it truly was and studying it on a daily basis for many years, I came to a divine fork in my road. I was presented with a decision by this most wonderful book that had become my long sought spiritual path. That decision was simple; keep believing in a world that was so obviously flawed or accept the possibility that there was something more. Most of us entertain a vague notion that maybe there is something better when we die or, if we still cling to the promise of worldly satisfaction, the possibility of happiness somewhere, somehow, sometime. But I had tried *somewhere*, *somehow*, and *sometime*, and they hadn't worked for me. Even with the love of a good woman and family, the hole in my soul was left unfilled. So I opened my mind to the possibility that maybe, just maybe, there was more, not just after I died, but here and now. *A Course in Miracles* presented me with just such an alternative and, being the commonsense, rational person that I am, I challenged it. I challenged it and the world at the same time. And you know what? It was simply put, no contest. I looked around at what the world had to offer and I saw nothing that endured, nothing that was fair to all of its inhabitants, and nothing that offered consistency or hope. The Course, on the other hand, offered all of these and more, much more. And as I pursued my intellectual and spiritual interrogation, it held up. What it presented me with challenged my entire belief system, the way I perceived the world, and my concept of reality. I am not a person prone to self-delusion but I realized that is exactly what I had done for my entire life; deluded myself into accepting a world where nothing held true, where change was inevitable and betrayed us at every turn, and a world where love, health, abundance, and satisfaction was reserved but for a few.

I have lived a relatively happy, healthy, and abundant life, so I have no axe to grind. But, in my latter years, I found I can no longer accept such a world as being the creation of a loving God. So I changed my mind. I changed my perception of reality and I changed my beliefs. And, judging from the fruits of my labors, I chose wisely. A year ago, those changes led me to the aforementioned fork in the road. From that decision point, I elected a reality that I could accept as true and would, I believe, bring me the complete happiness I had sought for so long. Once that decision was made, many things changed. My marriage got even better. In fact all of my relationships improved, including the one with my Creator. My life became fuller, richer, and more plentiful. And one night, without warning, I started to receive poetry. Those poems came from a place I had never known, a place never visited or conceived of. There, in that place, the book you are about to read, was born. It came as gift for me and I trust, for you as well. I hope you enjoy reading them as much as I have enjoyed receiving and writing them. They have been a blessing to me and it is my honor to share them with you.

One last word, a warning if you will. Contained within these pages are many messages. Some are stories, some are prayers, some are tongue-in-cheek, and some illuminate the absurdities of the world. I did not choose them, they chose me. Perhaps they will choose you as well.

The Emerald Mandala

Do not be afraid to enter
The Emerald Mandala
It's a sanctuary of sorts
It could end up nowhere
It could lead Home
We'll just have to immerse ourselves
See what we can learn
Visual pleasure to be sure
Deep green to get lost in
Gleam, sparkle, and intrigue
Enter the frontier of mind
Dare to search bravely
For answers that work
Solutions that hold true
Directions unforbidding
Signposts pointing towards Home

Conscious Denial

Cruel hand of fate deny me
The realness of any facts you project
I know the truth of the matter
Real indeed, it denies you too
Release firm grip on denial
Let truth find inroads
Let love clear the air
Deny all that surrounds us
Onward gaze go through it
Seeking the real world
The one touched gently by God
There lives nothing but truth
Nothing to deny or die for
Eternal life given freely
Denying only what lies between us

Large and Magnificent

I am no small matter
I refuse the puny portion offered
I will wait to feast with my King
Offer me no more refusals
When I reject those already proffered
I am great and holy and Christ
My brothers and sisters they join me
All as one we return
To golden palace offered
No more frail bodies
Nor brains impersonating Mind
No more flip flop emotions
Only peace and rest await us
Minus need or any wants
Whole and free and happy
Large and magnificent we are

Vocation Vacation

It's been a long time coming
This calling I now call my own
Seems like I've been on protracted vacation
All preparation for coming Home

Now my life begins anew
The reason for which I am sent
Nothing to be ashamed of
Nothing left to repent

Holy Father, guide me surely
The task too valuable to conceal
Naked and open before you
Too late to last appeal

The time has come to truly live
Lived truly until the end
Day will come when I lay body down
Gently, happily, I face my Friend
Brother Christ to welcome me in

The Healing

Emerald green color of healing
A mere symbol to be sure
Yet signal to mind of its coming
Accepted now, destined to be pure

Home found and place for work
The body not even considered
The mind is where healing is needed
Thoughts and concepts gone awry
Fixed in belief and illusion
Apart from Mind so holy
Cause of pain and worry

The mind once healed will carry
Blessings to all who attend
To those who listen carefully
To Holy Mind that never ends

Spirit and Mind immortal
Form no longer sole companion
The search for eternity ended
Son of God found and befriended

We Three

Let only two mourn me
When my passing comes to pass
For I have given them my best
Yet poorly served the rest

My heart belongs to you all
Boundless family we are
Angelic song for the ages
Carry us along together well

Slight of hand and camera obscura
Seem to interrupt life well lived
Simply a moment of blindness
Healed upon Heaven's receipt

But let not you two mend long
For with you I will always abide
Wholeness uninterruptible
You, me, we three (inviolate)
Forever joined, forever free

Unspeakable

Words can do love no justice
Symbols pale in its presence
So much more than we need say

No container large enough
No phrases sweet enough
The world becomes pointless
Except as point of receipt

Only flowers and other beauty
May speak to its loveliness
In words the pure of heart understand
Obviating all else around it

Nothing here worthy of exchange
Yet love belongs to us all
Gifted free and eternal
Waiting to be embraced

Let fall all other things
That have no value as love
Receive the one gift offered
Gently offered from Heaven above

Holding the Pen

I hold a certain bent
From this personality I'm in
I'm quite sure it colors these lines
But I hope I've made it perfectly clear
I step aside for all that delivers me
Never could I filter or delay it
Mine only to admire in passage
Gifts given us all together
I merely hold the pen

Eventual Demise

Give the lesser mind
No lease or leash
Stop it dead in its tracks
The lesser for the greater
Is rarely a good deal
But seal those corners
And mind those cracks
It denies itself never so well
But tame it in time we will
Let Mind take residence solely
We diminish ourselves otherwise
And progress ever so slowly
And insist on eventual demise

Favorite Words

Spoken in innocence they kindle
Love's warm fire within me
Like taking God's Hand in mine
Connected in every way possible
Divine touching the divine
Sweetness and love unteachable
Granting me audience once more
Saying those dearest of words
I love you papa

My Course

I consume a pearl
Each and every day
Dispensed from book of wisdom
My Brother speaks to me this way

No longer just facts or pathway
His voice emanates from pages pure
Teaching me all I need to know
Holding my hand, soothing my soul

Cover now worn, letters missing
Binding in need of mending
Yet nothing can diminish its truth
Nothing can take it away
My course has always been presented
By books and words that pray
But none so dear or precious
At holy tome bestowed by Jesus
Guiding light and bridge to Heaven
Instructions for minds long lost

Of a Single Density

Beauty hence torn away
From earth so tightly bound
Wanting so much to be born
Of a single density found
Pulled from dust finely ground
Light as air freed from sound
Chains held for ages uncounted
Letting love be about and abound
Heavy matter holding down its captor
The dove of peace seeks its home
Emerging from refuse
Refusing to be held down
Rejecting its right to be denied
Its rightful place in Heaven
Shaking off all restraints
Born anew, nothing faint

Much to Gain

O joy, you have not left me
For a moment my heart did die
Half believing our love was over
The finest of my life gone by
And then you lifted my pen
Placed it to paper once more
As if to say nay to despondency
Ever by my side you will be
My soul soars again on eagle's trail
My purpose still unspent
The joy given remains the same
Much work to do
So much to gain

Vortex Spit

Give me Thine words
Let none be my own
Let loose all to be captured
On pages betwixt and between
All to be shared freely
Mind streams running together
To pool in ocean of thought
Pure and undefiled by man
Wisdom to save us again
From ego trap re-defended
Pulling free this time around
Spit out from evil vortex
Into light and glory found

A Maker's Dozen

It's not for me to judge you, sister
I know now the mothering way
Felt in a moment of agony
Believing my babies lost one day

I did judge you briefly sister
Then Christ returned to order
Better thoughts to consider

I know now it is but love extending
No evil seen, no evil found
Perception makes of you an enemy
That threatens ego's bounds

Brother now hating brother
Stopping love's ebb and flow
Yet bear up, dear sister
And know your Help is so

It's simply that you love dear babies
Set your direction and go
In time to your own beat
Live bravely and let it be so

All the Same

My brother comes in many forms
Old men and fat ladies first
Short and tall, cute and small
Related we are, I love them all

Mind balloons bent to different shapes
Each to lend a tale
And expose within our hearts
The story that each will tell
And why it keeps us apart

Tis sad it is and most telling
Of what has bound us so
Leaves a trail less endearing
Than where our lives can go

Ignore the form, dear brother
Embrace each other proudly
With open heart, let love see
What lies within us
Is all the same, you see
All in Christ we be

Center's Heart

Some day I will write my farewell
As I lay at death's door
No longer do I fear it
For I know there is more
More to life than briefly lived
On this orb and place we call home
My mind now so confident
Of where I go from here
To my true Home, where I will stay
Next to my Brother and King
Never again tempted to stray
Never again to be seen apart
From Heaven's glow and Center's Heart

Most of All

I thank You, Father
For all that You do
I thank You for the Holy Spirit
For what He has done, and does, and will do
I thank You for sweet Jesus
And all He has done, and does, and will do
And all my brothers in Christ
For what they are to You
But most of all, dear Father
I love You

Fool's Errand

Free will, our best friend and enemy
Freedom's breast at best
Choice to depart, a tragedy
To leave our clan behind
The Holy Family, the only family
Orphaned for a time
Given leave to take a leave
If our soul so desired
The one decision best left alone
For to take leave of everything
A fool's errand to be sure

Absolutely Pure

I'm working with the Big Guy these days
Not sure I need a second job
I'll hang around and wait for signals
To see if retirement is still off

I should love what I do
And do what I love
Put them together, put me in love

The one thing I know
Is how little I know
So I'm deferring this decision
To someone in the know
A man's best advisor, to be sure
Holding the map book to Heaven
The One absolutely pure

So

Father
I never thought we would
Talk so freely
That I could touch Your Face
So lightly
Open up heart and mind
To see so clearly
To stand so close to Perfection
And love it so much

By Way of J

Lots of stuff keeps coming
Delivered at the oddest of times
Slipping in under the covers
To see if I can come play
Holy blessings, to be sure
Gifts of love surrounded
Slim idea of point of origin
Guessing, the best I can say
I know only their wonderment
And that they came
By way of J

Singing Love

From a place long forgotten
An ancient hymn comes through
Touching my heart with love
Meant for me and you
One we sang together
Many long time ago
Our voices merged as one
No single note discernable
The angelic choir, our accompaniment
The universe, our stage
Singing love to our Father
Singing love to each other
Singing love to All
Perfection of voice and music
Singing endlessly the call
To brothers lost and sisters worn
To bring them Home et al

Brothers Forever

No matter what he says
No matter what he does
I will take no aim at my brother
I will defend myself no more
Nor will slings and arrows
Drive from his door
I will love him without restraint
I will treasure him everyone
No longer can I harm him
My brother forever more

Something Worth Talking About

It seems like I've been waiting
All my life
To find something
Worth talking about

The more I know about
The things that truly matter
The less inclined I am
To spend the time
Or to take due notice
Of things better off
Left to dissolve

But now I approach truth
It astounds me quite greatly
I'm finally done waiting
Something worth talking about
Turns out to be silence

A Struggling Time

A time of soul unrest
Peace eludes, fear knocks
Doubt in various forms
Seeking to push love out
A call for strength goes out
A plea to sooth the soul
Peace again, dear Father
I know what I want
I know what I don't want
The choice is painfully clear
Bring me Home Beloved
Let the struggling end be near

The Body is Nothing

The body is nothing
Created in error
Sustained by belief
An attempt to be our own god
Now honored and worshipped
In true Creator's place
This symbol of separation
Defying oneness for its race
Lying to our eyes and ears
Singing ego's lament

As light breaks darkness
So shall faith eliminate the false
Some clear day ahead
Shall we know our brother's truth
That we are all the same
That lying behind the body illusion
The Spirit and Mind that bears
The stamp of what truly exists
Our Father God, always there

Staying Blind

The obvious eludes me so often
I can barely see what is before me
The truth so evident it blinds me
The world I see in its stead
When inward touch dispels it
I am amazed how easily I missed it
Love never lies or disguises
Truth seeking its place in mind
Only the obstacles before us
Deafen and keep us blind

A Dark Idea Diffused

I will no longer deny oneness
By admitting to separate things
My vision split, become as one
The senses, no fences detect

Blinding truth, eyes no longer needed
Clear insight never hindering
Passage of love within
Darkness no longer an issue
Sin, a dark idea diffused
Nothing but yes need matter
To put our soul to use

As new visual aids are imparted
To see past ego's way
The sight returns as single eye
Forgiving the need to stay
Covered by blanket of lightness
Sending dark ideas departing
No longer in my way

I'll Live Until I Don't

I'll live until I don't
Then we'll see what happens

The Greatest Lie

The greatest lie
Is that we sinned
We didn't

Dignity

Do not hide from thee
Behind thy dignity

Dark Corners

I still have dark corners
Where I fight
Battles within myself
A sucker punch
From out of nowhere
Sends me reeling
And struggling to stay afoot
Winning some, losing some
My beloved Friend urges me on
As ways and means are provided
To fight the good fight
Until it ends
To drop my hands
And extend them to save
Both me and my holy brother
Together, in light bathed

Masquerade

Christ masquerading as Sasha
And Chris, and all whom I see
Personality, looks, and means
Determine what we pretend to be
An endless parade of deception
A parlor game of dubious repute
Visually trying to confuse us
To shape and mold what we see
Into bubbles of resistance
Struggling to be free
Smote my ears
Sear mine eyes
Eliminate perception
Sweep bias away with truth
Let nothing form my dream
Let me see clearly of you
Nothing visible but knowledge found
Clearing my field of vision
Revealing love's sweet sound

No Fear

Forbid it entry
Deny it audience
An enemy awaits acquiescence
Assigning doubt as agent

Illuminate the domain of mind
Leave no dark corners unanswered
Sweep it away with holy will

Darkness always departs the room
When light becomes resident within

Towards Beauty

The impulse towards beauty
Elevates the mind
And calls us Home
Leaving debris unanswered
And ugliness to fend for itself
Yet nothing within
Leaves the call unanswered
Though restrained by the world we be
The call to Source and Heaven
Beckons our sight to foresee
Beyond all salty appearances
The Home where we may be
Oblivious to worldly strain
Towards beauty everlasting
The truth that makes us sane

Let Me See

Let me see no people
Nor bodies clothed in finery
Let me see no separation
Nor things that clash and bang
Let me see no animosity
Nor brothers hanging brother
From the tree I do not see
Let blindness rule my day
Let all that would convince me
Of world of opposites, I pray
To let me see only oneness
And Christ in all I survey
To never again see my brother
In any other way

Little or Nothing to Pay

From the Mind of Christ
To the hand of man
Exquisite pearls delivered
To trace the holy plan
From Heart of God
To sterling man
Endpoint beyond reality
The body bent far too much
Yet here we reside
And here we should say
Whatever delivers our senses
Seems to only delay
For Word of God delivered
Leaves little or nothing to pay

A Willing Part of the Whole

A willing participant I am
In the work of becoming the Whole
Straighter to fly inside
Less time spent all around
Seeking the Entirety that claims us
Beckoning starting from afar
The desire for fire, the urge to merge
A natural response truly given

At Love's Simple Request

As near as words can say
The idea constrained somewhat
Impulse clearly given
Perception the villain here

Truth tends to get covered
By the best of man's intent
Purity strained through a filter
Leaves less than originally spent

The meaning may stray
Along lashes of memory
Yet the heart remains pure
And needs no lovely requisite
Merely open to the delivery
At love's simple request

Casey's Game

From generation to generation
We teach the beloved game
Of batters and runners and such
To see sweet joy on the faces
As buckled youth rises to fame

The sound of the bat
As it greets intended ball
Driven through air and grass and dirt
Pursued by the chosen fielder
Excitement moving in but one direction
Exchange of ball to glove to hand
Now soaring through air again
Seeking to find convergence
Somewhere on the other end

The ball pops mitt
An ounce before arrival
The batter is out
The game is won
We all go home the better

Chains of Our Own Making

Self imposed, self restricted
The chains we wrap and own
To impose the lonely exile
So assume the position prone
Let defeat stand atop you
Pushing the mind to madness
To sedate the lonely coup
Paying attention to all that commands
That we chain ourselves to belief in man
Ignore the holy reality
In favor of sex and ham
So very hard it is in the taking
To lock our chains
And keep on faking

A Bolt Once Thrown

It's all one thing
Rejoined that never departed
Moving parts appear lithely
False impressions all around
Separate things grant no pardon
A bolt once thrown
Is never forgotten
Yet true to form we remain
No reason to go one better
Until we see the light
That reveals whatever mattered

Nowhere Outside Heaven

To us together
I raise my cup
Brothers reformed
Come back together
Forever more
Twins departed
Headed for the door
Went through wily threshold
Only to find no more
Nowhere outside Heaven
Nothing apart from The Core

The World's Fool

Children at play
On this lovely day
Excitement and joy abound
Unbridled energy in body found

But never do they concede
To anything less than impossible
Until we limit their limits
And state of what not they're able
They grow and learn
To be far less
Than ever imagined knowable
To limit the expression of joy
Becomes our fear repressible
To give up on who we are
To make our souls unredeemable

Give up instead
On the notion of limits
Take on the world and its rules
And never be deemed its fool

Poet's Quarter

I enter my final quarter
I shall live to eighty, no more
Other lives lived in other fashion
The first three quarters born

Brainiac and shy to start with
Later fluid athlete arrives
Finally golden boy with stiff penis
Trying so hard to thrive

Survived these three
I did somehow
Poet man I now admire
Standing here taking my place

I soon depart with Christ
To live yet another life
That last lovely quarter owed
To complete the divine price

I Speak Only of You

I speak only of You, dear Father
My words owe nothing less
A waste they are of anything else
Nowhere else will I invest
My time or effort found wanting
Only if not what I profess
My heart belongs to You, Beloved
My mind attends the rest
Until such time as warrants
My return to You, holy blessed

Freedom's Press

Laugh and joy
Partners in sanity's pool
Born to keep us together
Born to make us fools
Yet happy fools we may be
If we yield to freedom's press
And leave behind false dignity
And settle for nothing less

Always on Time

The last vestiges are gone
Of guilt and shame left homeless
By my heart's reform at hand
No longer judging my brother
No longer afraid to die
Never again to condemn or justify
My fate hard pressed to explain
All that has bought me here
But never will again
My soul no longer restless
I know what waits ahead
My time here now tempered
By what my heart has said
The words I leave in memory
Of conversations sweetly had
In one-on-ones with my Brother
My heart to His
His soul to mine
Reunited but never parted
Late, but always on time

Waiting

I am yours, Father
I wait to be claimed
Openly and joyfully I wait
My soul singing to be claimed

So long have I waited
So much have I wasted
In time's lonely shelter
Waiting to be claimed

The time is near, but never fear
For I wait with yearning heart
Content to do what is necessary
Until sweet time to depart

Hot Off the Press

The words now gently delivered
In form of book they are placed
In the hands of brothers most capable
To deliver to those oppressed
By faint hearts with nothing to hope for
By souls who have welcomed less
Now to arrive as promised
To welcome them Home at last

Divine Fortunes Untold

To grow unattended
Seems a perilous fate
Alone in the middle of oneness
Seems a mite out of place
No need to staunchly remain
In fixed position born of need
Observe the fullness before you
The welcoming committee to greet
Brothers and sisters adorn you
Sparkling diamond, of which you are whole
Calls out and secures your position
Amid divine fortunes untold

Elusive Rhyme

I watch brilliance emerge
As part of my day
A bit of a mismatch
For the rest of the day
Regardless of ratio
I live for the time
When pen touches paper
To bring the elusive rhyme

Magic Flute

I play the magic flute
The one that makes no sound
Command performance requested
With no one else around
Celestial music, the fare
The score no less than divine
The instrument a thing of love
Placed to my lips, I surrender
To the sound that must be heard
No ears attend my music
No eyes to see me perform
Silent notes easily departing
From Source to hearts that know
Of Heaven's love for us
Carried in music so fair
Destined to touch our souls
Hoping to carry us where
The dawn is always rising
Where the sun will never depart
To a land of never darkness
To the Home within our hearts

I Make No Apologies

I make no apologies
For deliveries bestowed
Of precious gems of wisdom
For each of us to behold
I lay no claim to fortune
Fame appeals me not
I have no need of freedom
That, I've already got
All of me invested, everything to gain
The whole of me delivered
To unite with you again

As Gentle as Jesus

My life, my goal to be
Nowhere in the near vicinity
Far beyond the eagle's prey
Searching, still searching
For a lively place to stay
My goal to be
My life to come
To touch my brother gently
As life will bring to such
To be as gentle as Jesus
To convey His beloved touch

Guilt Jail

I accept guilt no longer
Nor admit its handmaiden pain
Both intended to deliver
Nothing of any gain
Imposing limits unneeded
Agents of illusion giving reign
To symbols of separation
That weigh and tighten our chains
Admitting us only as prisoner
Keeping us lowly without love
Closing the doors to Heaven
Denying the truth above
Yet have no fear, my brother
For fear is not our master
We have the power to deny it all
To pin it down and let it fall
To let illusion no longer prosper
By denying us the one true law
Assume brave posture, my brother
Disperse such falsity now
Come Home with given witness
Freed from jail to live our vows

Holy Family

I have hundreds of offspring
Gifted to me so far
I yield to thoughts born anew
I field varieties of questions
What will I name them
And who will I see
When eyes are finally opened
To approve the gathering to me
To know with utmost clarity
All begotten and raised by me
Precious infants so small
Compose my holy family
With brothers and Father of all

I, Not Me

I, not me
Speaking for the we
Have a few words to say
Two residents appear
To be one too many
There's the little me
That's the one you usually see
Then there's the big I
The one that knows the truth to be
Having given leave much too long
Allowing little me to be
Much more of a participant
Than I would like him to be
I think I'll stage me a coup
See if I can get rid of him

Become the One

This is what we get together
Much more than sum of the parts
A feeling unlike any other
One that glows in the dark

A measure of man and woman
To see if we may leave
Separate gender identities
Behind, so that *we* may be

Dropping the diminutive
In exchange for the very large
Is not only smart money
But will captain us far

We'll never know this again
Lest sufficient effort be made
To drop away separate deceit
Become the One
We were meant to be

How I Do It

I know Him
That's how I know what to write
I don't really hear Him
I see far too little to see Him
I'm not taking direction, per se
We share the same Mind, at times
Knowing what I need to say

The Greybeards

I seek the greybeards for some reason
The motive is still unclear
Gravity pushing us down and together
Maybe the pain
Maybe the years

Some unrevealed parlance
Soon and where to take place
Connection to be established
To lead us to unknown fate

Yet I trust my Counselor
He never lets me down
If there's a need to blend us
Then by all means
Let's get down

If Only We Understood It

We yearn for the poetic
That richness is needed, is clear
The shallow substitute given
Is made of that less dear
We cognize of more
If only we would know it
We strive for more
If only we could show it
Brave words provided in defiance
If only we understood it

Faith to See

Doubt builds walls
Faith opens doors
I'd much rather go through
One with a bit of an opening

Foundation of crumbs
Product of fear responded
Doubt babies crowding ahead
Not giving us much to work with
Not leaving enough instead

Faith, on the other hand
Looks mighty good to me
Warm flowing delivery
Giving me eyes to see

The Best Map

We have a new way before us
A different notion of things to be
An ingenious way of imagining
A wondrous way to see

Pointing out new directions
Reciting from prose and verse
Spinning toward a more perfect union
Than has ever been rehearsed

Blink through watery veil
Strain to see the difference
That no one else can tell

Taking back that never given
Refuses to yield a lot
Let us take note of our future
Construct the best map we can plot

Never Look Back

My faith is back
I never thought I left
Until such time as favored
To see my sight bereft
Of clearer vision restored
Of mind veils dropped again
To hide the tear within
Created by lack of wisdom
Born from faith again
Once I had my *ah ha*
I remembered where I had been
My faith, or lack of it, we'll say
Made obvious my doubts in play
So I sucked it up
Got myself back on track
Things are looking much brighter now
No need to ever look back

Buckle Up Buttercup

Buckle up buttercup
The ride is about to begin
It could get bumpy ahead
So let's really strap us in
Tis a ride I've waited for long
I've finally paid my fare
Ready to assume what is offered
Ready to become quite paired
With my brother holding tightly beside me
Having finally learned how to care

Quite Right

His solutions are quite elegant
His work, a joy to behold
He assembles plans quite eloquent
Places for love to take hold
Moments of vital importance
Words sweetly beheld
Sights to amaze and astonish
It's quite wonderful I think
To see it done quite right

Times Left Blue

I boldly go
To what I need to know
To make this half-life livable
I sadly leave the dispensable
To life left holding the bag
It wasn't much true or visible
But at times I kind of liked it
Yet too many times left blue
With nothing of much to show for it

Colored in White

You color one part
I, the other
Pieces coming together
From far and wide
Mosaic shades assembled
The many into the One
All flowing limitless and free
Divine hues merging
Coloring soul in white, the fee

Jammin

Splendiferous, my friend
Simply splendiferous
Thanks for letting me be
A part of your mystery
Poetry paired to music
So fair to my ears
Caressing my heart
Settling in mind
Keep kickin out the hits Bobby
We be jammin together
Til the end of rhyme

Full Sails

The person who reads will choose
And decide what he must say
Perhaps, "this is appealing"
Maybe "what the hey"

The brother who utters the latter
Will put the book back
From whence it came
Step in another direction
To play a different game

I wish him well, he has my love
We will meet again some day
The others of you remaining
To you I have this to say

Welcome aboard dear mates
Grab an oar, yet hold it calmly
For now we know our fate
Full sails set for Home
We move at rapid rate

Attention to Innocence

I watch the children at play
The sight amazes me so
Flowing within each other
In a way to only be hoped
No conflict, no hate
All fitting together
As food on a plate
Feast served and eaten together
No crumbs or mess remain
They run and swing and pull together
To us, as adults, a conduct refrain
Take our lessons from young ones
Who inherit from us to hate
Pay attention to innocence
Never wait for too late

No Need to Travel

I have no need of travel
I've been there more than once
Seen it all, heard it all
Until it made no sense

I longed for Paris
The Coliseum intrigued me too
Until I learned of wisdom
Til I learned of me and you

Now I know the difference
Between going or staying here
Beauty, my friends, beholds *us*
And never need travel again

Mystery of Rhyme

I must confess, at times
I do not understand all rhyme
Yet I flow and carry
With the current of it
Feeling its surging sensation
The clarity of its tone
Stumped as far as using it
It affords no place to lodge
Still trying to make good sense of it
To be understood at large

Fading Laws

These laws do not suffice me
I know not from whence they came
Worldly bred from nothing
Constraints to keep bodies together
Barriers to keep souls apart
Upheld by beliefs unpardoned
Given life separation unfought
They are nothing, if not nothing
A failing to accept the crown
Of Christhood truly offered
By laws superior to these
Giving us leave to everything
No longer the world to appease

Incomplete Facts

Facts, facts, and facts
At least what we consider such
Fills our lives with falsity
Ideas born of incomplete thought
Manipulated and spun
Until the mix is just right
Truth traded for revenue dollars
Imposed throughout the night
Hard pressed on pages galore
Keep feeding on vagrant thoughts
Bar truth from entering yon door
Allow the world's press
To maintain our thirst for less
Clearly we settle for facts sensational
The preference to be entertained
Truth traded for that which plagues us
Imbedded in deep crevasse
Let us rise up, discard such trivia
Accept only truth at last

Leaving the Dream

Checkout time approaches
I'm all packed and ready to go
Just hanging out til my bus arrives
The one with no return, you know

It's been quite the adventure
These roles I've truly played
It's been an awful long time
Since we started this little charade

I stand tired of playing
My Home awaits me now
I'll be seeing you a little later
Don't dally, I'll miss you there

Cranky

I have been known
To be a bit cranky
That damn old ego
Keeps yanking my crank

Put in moods quite foul
I don't even like myself
He's starting to piss me off
I really don't like his stance

Enough of my life
Has been chewed and swallowed
It's starting to come back up
Might want to move aside my friend
For one, I promise, last time
Til ego butt is booted
Out the door, by rhyme

Beauty of the Thought

The beauty of the Thought
Is quite impressive, I'm sure
If only we could see it
It couldn't help but make us pure
Cleanse us of all we started
Purge us of all that's past
Minds cleaned from the inside out
Clarity at long last

Ego's Dirge

Strike up the band
Get those instruments tuned
Clear our throttled throats
Of all that blindly clogs us
Get ready to let it out
We're all done tuning up
For a farewell song of rote
We're about to lose an enemy
The only one of note

My Babies

I did them all as Waldo
In faint years gone by
Odes and poems, my favorites
All I could see without eyes

They are all fair children
Together again
Poised and ready to join
The family formerly christened
As duty and friend of man

Still quite lovely
As blossom atop spring tree
Fused to my heart forever
By offspring returned to me

Daily Bread

The thoughts profound
The language elegant
Born of holy care
The meaning quite eloquent
Please take me there
Let me curl up lovingly
Inside each born eternally
Within the sound and rhyme
Going with the rhythm
Attempting to stay in time
Yet timeless they are
Holy they are bred
Consistently inside us
Daily, our bread

The Golden Ring

Waldo, my friend
We search within
To look for joy or love
Hoping for this or such
Bestowed from God above
What else but truly counts
And makes for wisest choice
It really doesn't seem to matter
To whatever we give our voice
The whole of it waits in silence
Requiring no mandated toll
Inherited for next to nothing
Peace and silence, our goal
To stand in quiet murmur
Next to our Lord and King
Participant in holy wedding
The love, our golden ring

Normal Sanctuary

I did not know
The depth of the man
Until I made full review
Ignoring the outside presented
To view and look through
Got past the eyes and face
Refused the other parts
Intent on only seeing
What lived within his heart
Once I found it
I was both startled and amazed
At what I found inside him
Surrounded by formal grace
The beloved redeemer we seek
Hides beneath the form
Be blind to all that is visible
Finding sanctuary from the norm

Full Attendance

See us all with innocence
Behold the holy Whole
Beyond all rhyme or reason
Stand as naught but soul
Making ourselves fit and ready
To meet the holy groom
To walk with exquisite bride
Full attendance at the communion
Everyone wants to go Home
Everyone wants to be One

Lack of Contrivance

There is no contrivance here
No phony baloney for sure
Zero to cover or conceal
All but fare for the feast
Let crumble all that be false
Let fall and fade away
Nothing left good to get from it
Might as well let it stray
To where it is and where we pay
A fare much too high
A ticket too extravagant
Be naked instead
Bare soul in wind and sun
Reach out to bare brother
Be uncontrived as One

Light Breezes

I walk lightly upon the earth
Neither tangling nor tripping
Just touching, lightly touching
The breeze upon your crown
Coming to less to achieve the more
Still hanging around
My feet on the floor
Yet time will change the schedule
Periods to stay, instants to go
Brushing briefly past the story
With nowhere else to go
Absorbing each other
A most splendid way to go
Breezes illuminating the way
Making light so

Nothing Left to Say

Father, the more I pray
The less words I say
You already know it all
You know who I am
And who I will be
There's little left to say
Except my heart's true way
Speak to me Blessed Father
As I to You
In so many ways
Words changing to love
Leaving nothing left to say

Lost Without You

Beloved Holy Spirit
Once again, I come to you
To ask what is always given
To accept that you do

I ask for your daily guidance
In all that I must do
And for your loving judgment
Instead of any I deem true

Requesting your part in decisions
So holy they must ring true
I know, without your direction
Lost I would be without you

Our Best

Christ Jesus of long ago
Patiently waiting forever
If brothers need you to
Counted among the fortunate
Those never to be split in two
You have been my truest friend
Encompassing all the rest
The ones you give your heart to
The ones who try their best
Those who would flounder
And never find you
Without the holy quest
Beloved brother, friend forever
Showing us our best

Multicolored Space

Gifts of love bestowed
Appearing in various form
We see the same in many ways
All separate rays returning
To the same divine Sun

We do so many fine things alike
Signs of brotherhood designed
We love, honor, respect
We appreciate, enjoy, and care
We devote, imbue, and praise
The holy within all things

Simply God showing us His Face
Letting love reveal itself
In multicolored space

Genius in Many Forms

Christ Mind is brilliant
Showing genius in many forms
The mind of Einstein
To a ceiling within a church

From words wisely spoken
To swallows in a row
The Place is simply amazing
No denial of where to go

The creative process alive and well
In the care of hands most holy
Stunning us with its brilliance
Showing far more than we know

It's not likely done with us yet
Many a form to attend within
The Mind that forever amazes
And truly will never end

Me2

My good friend and brother
Waldo, for short
Penned this ode to stardom
One I will ever report

He like me is not too proud
To be the poet of the crowd

I owe you one, good buddy
I like it very much
I think I'll try to use it
Thank you for the touch

Two Guests

Two guests, we entertain
One a friend, the other a fool
The friend brings glad tidings
The fool cares but for itself

The friend, a worthy house guest
No room for the fool at all
Both are thoughts, my friend
Resident in the mind of man

One is love and born of God
The other, a tenant banned
The friend brings truth of oneness
The other proclaims detachment

In oneness lies safety and peace
The lie holds nothing of worth
Born of false perception
Confirmed by senses and beliefs
Maintaining the general illusion
That we are less than we be

The guest of union, our truth and friend
The other, bereft of all
Let us choose carefully our guest list
Lest we settle for nothing at all

Difficult it is to see beyond illusion
Close as the nose on our face
Yet deny senses and false belief
Let them limit us no more
Discard the chains of separation
Let only truth come through our door

Home Song

This is the song I sing
This is the music I play
Rendered from fountain's pen
In words ordained to say
Lyrics born of angels
Tunes played throughout the day
Melody strewn with ashes
Of old life traded for new
Echoing throughout eternity
Reverberating its way through
The sound will travel forever
Arriving at purpose true

Unlimited Field and Stream

Wildflowers that grace our mind
Are but thoughts colored well
Gathered together in love bouquet
Deliver them gently to my cell
I would gather them in profusion
I would deliver them then to you
Stretch, burst out of brain box
Into the field of dreams
From there it is but a dance away
To unlimited field and stream

Captain of the Oar

My crew of brothers with me
My Captain at the helm
Braving stormy waters
Slicing through the sea
Searching for a view of Heaven
And the peace at which we'll be
Trusted well, loved even more
The Captain shields us all
The crew has taken to oar
Pulling hard with all our might
To voyage away no more

Love Delivered

To be this blessed
Is my joy, my sweet joy
Unimagined since birth
Unknown to employ
To have a heart once so empty
Now at burst point to be
Tis love sweet brother
Come share it with me
Our Father delivers it endlessly

Table Laid Lightly

The table laid lightly
White linen and silver spoon
Finest of china available
To grace the lovely room
The feast but awaits arrival
Of the One who brings it all
And lays it upon our table
A feast for one and all

Portrait of the Whole

Elegantly simple
Simply elegant
The beauty of the solution
Quite wonderful to see
Poetry in motion
Rainbow sketching the sky
Complete bed of flowers
The what and the why
Eternally gracing us
With vision quite high
A palette of unknown delights
Colors to warm the soul
Beauty unimaginable
Portrait of the Whole

Street Smart

It's the part of me known to few
The kid from the streets
Of town coldly cruel
From the darkness and cold
To the light and warm glow
Of Heaven on earth
In Rocky Mountain gold
It's part of me still
Likely to reappear
In words rightly rendered
It's the ruffian reformed
It's the street smart part
So temper your judgment
Of me and my words
Knowing I am quite likely
To put you off in turn
It really hardly matters
They're just words, of course
We are still but lonely brothers
Without words of course

Far Less Separation

The plan of convergence
Remains a mystery to me
I witness the signs of its coming
Yet not clear enough to see

I trust completely the planner
I've seen His work before
A master of subtlety indeed
Owner of Mind unfathomable
Fairly well equipped to succeed

I'll likely step up and participate
I know a winner when I see one
I see no better way to turn
Looks like I'm in for the haul
All of us coming together
Far less separation to forestall

Journey Unlike the Rest

We will leave no soul behind
We're all in this together
The One regaining Itself
Breaking loose equivalent tether
Evacuate this world we will
Leave it in the dust
Homeward bound for so much more
Our journey holy blessed
Our destination unlike the rest
Home within our Father
Home again at last

Song of Prayer

I wish to add my voice
To the choir that sings to Heaven
The joyful sounds of brothers
United in voice as one
No worldly cares to pay
Nothing to get in our way
Of joining in love and music
Singing our fears away
Hearts no longer burdened
Hate no longer considered
Love our only choice
To carry our voices this way
Arriving at the gates of Heaven
Just in time for the holy day
The one we waited for so long
The one that we kept at bay
No longer will we fear it
We sing with love to pray
Unified voice opens the gate
And God invites us to stay

Til I Die

For the rest of my life
All I need do
Is keep on pushing this pen
Continuing to write for you
A happy dream it will be
The one finally coming true
To be of service to my Father
To be directed by Holy Spirit
To work as one with my Brother
To move the pen til I die

The Imaginerium

The Imaginerium is open for play
Come to spend an hour
Come to spend the day
It's really quite wonderful
You don't even need to pay
It's grand and it's free
Available to all
Come take sight of it with me
Let us revel until we call
The place by its righteous name
Paradise through the looking glass
The one of Heavenly fame

Integrating in Time

I lose nothing
By giving it away
The nature of it holy
The size uncontained
Attempts to capture it
Will fail from the start
Far too much for one of us
We need only be part
Of the wondrous love
Washing over us
The light that trues the mind
Simply becoming us
Integrating in time

Part and Parcel

I resist analysis
It decrements the whole
Of ideas entirely presented
I would rather enjoy it completely
Or simply not at all
I've settled for the partial
For way too long
I seek now only the Whole
The part and parcel appeal me
I think I'll make it Home

We

I will be your teacher
And you will be mine
Together we will learn of truth
And the path that is divine

We will pierce the darkness together
We will part the clouds as one
Seeking the sun upon our faces
Accepting our fate post partum
Knowing rebirth has begun

We are inseparable, my brother
Our Father having but one Son
We are that Son together
We are the favored One
We are the Sun of Heaven
Our journey all but done

Departed

Home is in sight now
Darkness fading at long last
The sun shining brightly ahead
The feast denies the fast
All our Father offers
Appears in fullness cast
Laid out on golden path
My heart stretches to touch it
My mind opens to take it in
All gifts surely imparted
All given that lay within
Faith now turned to knowledge
Doubt cast out the door
Confirmation no longer needed
Knowing what I knew before
The gift originally given
Ere I departed Heaven's door

The Futile Joining of Two

The joining of two in body
The pleasure quite extreme
Two sides of the same illusion
Coming together it seems
Giving the appearance of oneness
When in fact it can never be true
The futile joining of bodies
Is but giving the dream its due
The striving to keep up the delusion
And body organs so frail
Using blue pills and horny thoughts
To maintain the constant flail
We bang them together
These bodies we call our home
Yet ever they leave us lonely
Far from oneness atoned
Let the race die out
And what will be left
No bodies to keep us apart
Leaving Spirit uncleft

The Constant Challenging of Reality

The constant challenging of reality
Is exercise and time well spent
For know we not where we truly live
And to whom we pay our rent

A bottled up world to be sure
No freedom or wholeness found
Push the walls of illusion
Til nothing but Spirit abounds

A cage of thoughts and beliefs
Giving the world its fuel
Allowing ego to be ruler
O'er the land of the dual

Yet only one can be truly you
And ruled by Master most wise
Who alone shows what is true
As seen through Paradise eyes

Mon Frere

Thank you, Mon Frere
For the geese in timely unison
And the butterfly in air
To the mountains so fair
Spacious blue skies, my canvas
To paint upon the day
With sunrise golden glitter
That brings me round to say
I am but truly grateful
Thank You, Mon Frere, for today

Amid the Joy

This is my job
This is my calling
Journey it I shall
Love to keep me from falling

Each moment is joy
Each letter a gem
Every word in every sentence
Brings me closer to Him

Never did my life envision
The work that became my joy
Little else matters now
Except love amid the joy

Holy Grail

My newfound friends and I
Deny the worst case scenario
We deal in only best case
It would be quite silly
To think not so

We get what we ask for
And nothing more, or less, in life
Paradise given, if requested
Or days of pain and strife

Yours, my friend, for the asking
Choose wisely or certainly fail
To get that truly deserved
To achieve the Holy Grail

Sight Bereft

I go between the lines
Unless there's a reason not to
Why waste that precious effort
On something not worth the time
Many more things to consider
Important matters left to redress
Certain articles of clothing
Used to cover our best
Skin and bones aplenty
Fabrics to cover even that
More layers of identity proclaimed
Sightless to see beneath
All those things to consider
In place of all that is left
A Mind and Spirit uncovered
With nothing but sight bereft

It

The writing
The reading
The spelling of it
Leave me all but consumed
With the breadth of it
The absolute miracle of it
A lone dove recently departed
From hold of world dissented
Combining with the Source of it
Spiritually born to tailor-fit it

The Size of the Gift

There is no sacrifice
Nor insufficiency as such
Scarcity only in the viewing
Of but a small part
Of which we have much

The size of the gift restrained
Only by depth of belief
That tries to put a choke hold
On the trust that provides relief

Be only willing to deserve it
To know in your mind it is so
Pieces are just not acceptable
When we freely partake of the Whole

Without Life's Pain

Love holds the universe together
Invisible oneness in all
Magnificent Mind of God
Enveloping all of creation

We make nothing of our own
Everything real is undivided
Nothing owned in separate
All a part of the Whole

Nothing to want or need
Nothing gained or lost
All in the All take part
Without limits or strain
Simply being what is
Without life's pain

The Flower

Love leaves room
On flower unpetaled
To grow fair leaves
With softer mettle

Beauty unrestrained
Amid sweet bloom
Foretelling our pleasure
Denying our doom

A hint of rosemary
Fragrance to tempt our eyes
To see that deeply hidden
The flower amid the prize

Be Remembered

Be remembered
Get your name on an ink pen
Immortality assured
To the length of the refill

Time is running out, my friend
Get your head in the game
The option exists
To be known as One
Or not of any fame

The One From the Two

Some day soon
The light will come
To show us the way
To reunite the One
Illuminating the path before us
Demonstrating the life we have led
Re-membering our members
The One from the many instead

Become Golden Hearted

This is as home as I get
For now, at least
Transient though I may be
For me, simply a stopover
I'm daring to be free

We'll be pals for awhile
As I stay to take care of business
Eventually, we need to drop it
And come back to our senses

Pals imply we're apart
Nothing could be farther away
From the truth newly imparted
So let's pack up and leave
As the One we departed
Come with me brother
To become golden hearted

Heaven's Milk

I realize the contradiction
I can envision how it appears
I seem to consume much more
Than worldly lot, I fear
Deny it, I will, to the end
Even whilst taking a bite
I need a little nourishment
A little manna for the trip
That will put me on a diet
Of Heaven's milk I sip

From the Past

Some day it will arrive
Point of convergence defined
We will stand and cheer together
While they strike up
The Heavenly band
Secret tone to open the door
Sweet rhyme to call at last
We are the Christ
We are the One
Finally arriving together
From long being lost in past

We Choose

Fueled by guilt
I choose the pain
A thought wholly accepted
To punish the fallen me

Choosing the illusion
Of body controlling mind
Confusing cause and effect
Letting the mind lag behind

Yet the body but follows
Instruction from deep within
Ignited by guilt and fear
To appease the imagined sin

We hold the key, dear brothers
To pain and disease uncovered
We choose what we get
Then give it away
To causes we refuse to know
We hold the key to wellness
In our mind, waiting to be so

Chest of Gold

I choose to remain in chains
I choose to welcome pain
I choose all that happens
That seems to be of no gain

Yet the choice is mine to make
What I give is what I take
No matter what form it takes

I have yielded to helplessness
I have given my power away
To satisfy a greedy ego
Trying to keep me where it may

But I am Christ
I kneel to none but the best
I decide now to choose anew
And decline all the rest

Only the ego will now die and suffer
For I refuse its evil quest
Accepting now only the treasure
I open the buried chest
Given at birth to Christ of old
It contains but gold, I'm told

The Answer

The only thing preventing healing
Is accepting the answer proffered
We can pray all we want
And nothing will happen
Until we deny the fear offered
And deny that guilt is real
We stand no chance of healing
Until they lose their appeal
Yet hope will reign forever
We will never be set aside
From our Father's Holy Love
That waits for us while we hide
Ask and have faith in the answer
For truly it will come
If we but open our heart and mind
And welcome it, to heal as One

No Pain, My Gain

I refuse to accept the pain
Let ego no longer rule
No matter how many prescriptions
It tenders to its fools

I refuse the placebo offered
To take the place of pain
Giving away the power
Of my mind to choose again
To rule the body
Instead of the other way around

So I decline the remedies
Accept only what is true
I no longer need their enmity
Only faith will pay my due

I deserve far more than given
By slovenly master reigned
Who gave me nothing but heartache
Revealing it through the pain
That what was offered was nothing
That now becomes my gain

Places Outside the Origin

Everywhere I've placed the pain
Letting it lodge with nothing to gain
My legs, my hands, my head
Sickness or infirmity my bed

Always outward to body
Always given away
To places outside the origin
Hoping they would stay

To avoid the recognition
That from mind they truly came
These troubles and trappings
That offered up my pain

Step aside now false god
I give you leave no more
To rule my life or being
I reject you from my door
Never again will you guide me
Free from tyranny evermore

I Awake This Morning

This morning I awake
To my prayer long answered
Given the gift of truth
Illusion dispelled in its wake

I asked to be healed
Of sundry ills imposed
Lacking faith in its coming
I search through pills and prose

I awake this morning
To the simplest truth
Long offered yet never accepted
Avoiding the answer produced

Today, I accept it fully
Today, I awake to know
That truly what was offered
Was always mine to know

www.ingramcontent.com/pod-product-compliance
Lightning Source LLC
Chambersburg PA
CBHW072154270326
41930CB00011B/2419